Everyone Owns A

SHATTERED
MIRROR

Connie Raney

PRESS

Everyone Owns A Shattered Mirror
by Connie Raney

Printed in the United States of America

ISBN 9781498422734

www.xulonpress.com

TABLE OF CONTENTS

ACKNOWLEDGEMENTS

I want to first thank Jesus Christ for my salvation. All of this is only possible because of Him. I also want to thank everyone who has supported me in this healing journey. To all of you who have read this book, I pray that you have received a blessing. If you are struggling, I pray you will turn it over to God and let Him help you. If you haven't accepted His free gift of salvation (John 3:16), I pray you will. If you aren't sure how, here is a place to start.

The Roman Road

Romans 3:23
Romans 3:10
Romans 6:23
Romans 5:8
Romans 10:9-13

INTRODUCTION

Who would have thought a high school dropout and a wounded little girl looking for love, both from broken homes of alcoholic families, would today be a strong, loving couple, and successful business owners? That definitely wasn't what I saw coming in my future, but here we are, two separate lives that found wholeness in Christ and began serving Him together as a couple. Two lives joined together, happily married today with two wonderful children: a daughter, recently married to a remarkable man in the Navy, and a son, close to graduating high school, getting ready for his next big step in life.

Really, I believe only God knew. Although He was the farthest thing from our minds, He guarded and protected us, faithfully and steadily moving in the background of our lives for many years without us even knowing it. Despite our attempts to interfere with the plan God had mapped out for us, He was still at work, molding and shaping us according to His divine purpose.

During the most difficult years of our childhoods, and tremendous challenges in adulthood, we never dreamt that someday we would own several businesses with over 500 employees. We had no idea we would fulfill my husband Buddy's dream of living on a cattle ranch, or mine of owning a house in the Florida Keys. It was too much to dream, or even hope for, but God had a plan for us, and when we learned to trust Him, great things began to happen.

This is the story of a threefold cord, the story of us – God, Buddy, and me. Many times the storms of life have worn and frayed our spiritual braid, almost to the breaking point, but God always showed up, often in unexpected ways.

"And if one prevail against him, two shall withstand him; and a threefold cord is not quickly broken."
–Ecclesiastes 4:12

Chapter 1

MIRRORS DO SHATTER

Everyone owns a shattered mirror within themselves – a mirror reflecting the pain and sorrow over brokenness that has occurred in their lives -- broken toys, broken promises, broken relationships, and broken hearts. Each member of a family has a perceived image – a mirror -- of their family as a whole, as well as their individual place within it. However, mirrors within the heart of each family member shatter when something tragic such as divorce, illness, or other heartbreaking events, happens to the family relationship. Each person tries to put it back together, in their own way, but it is full of cracks and missing pieces. Everyone's mirror is not the same; the cracks are in different places; there are missing shards of glass that are preventing the mirror from being made whole. Even the seemingly tiniest of missing pieces sometimes create the biggest holes, which impact the rest of that person's life. Tragedy affects each family member differently, so I am writing from the viewpoint of my mirror, which is different from that of everyone else.

We all make choices in life. Those choices affect everyone around us, good or bad. We have to learn that no matter what our childhood was, or what our circumstances are now, God loves us and has a plan for our lives. It is never too late to make a change. We can change; we can be forgiven; and we can forgive.

If this book prevents at least one person from going down the same rugged, unstable path I was on, or they choose to accept Jesus as their Savior, it will be worth it all. Becoming transparent has been difficult for me. I'm convinced God has given me this desire, and it has been a healing process for me. Through all the pain, God has brought me peace.

"For the mountains shall depart, and the hills be removed; but My kindness shall not depart from thee, neither shall the covenant of My peace be removed, saith the Lord that hath mercy on thee." – Isaiah 54:10

I never expected to be writing a book. Not me. I am too private, too reserved. I have always worried about other people's perception of me. How could I share such personal, painful things about my life and me? What would people think of me? I used to cringe every time Buddy would share his testimony. I was nervous about how much detail he would share and what they would think.

I've kept a journal or diary since I was about thirteen years old. Journaling has always been my way of dealing with things. I could write my thoughts out on paper without feeling like I was exposing myself. So this book started out as a therapy journal, just a way to deal with my past and heal. The more I wrote, the more God kept telling me that someone needed to read my story. So here I am, writing a book. It is just my life, as I see it, and if the telling of my story helps at least one person who may be undergoing what may feel like insurmountable challenges, then it will be worth it.

I have experienced the pain of brokenness, but God has shown me that He doesn't discard the broken. He repairs and restores the disordered pieces of our lives into a divinely inspired mosaic. The experience of brokenness in our lives qualifies us to help provide comfort to somebody else, just as the Apostle Paul wrote:

"Blessed be God, even the Father of our Lord Jesus Christ, the Father of mercies, and the God of all Comfort; Who comforteth us in all our tribulation, that we may be able to comfort them which are in any trouble, by the comfort wherewith we ourselves are comforted of God."–2 Corinthians 1:3-4

Chapter 2

MY CRACKS

I was born and lived in Hialeah, Florida until I was seven years old. I have good memories of the time there. One particular memory that stands out was walking to the playground at the elementary school with my grandmother. We would sit at the picnic tables and put puzzles together as we waited for my older sister to get out of school. I recall spending a lot of time playing outside. When we later moved to Green Cove Springs, Florida, I was excited to see woods on two sides of the house. I was definitely a tomboy and loved being outside.

My younger sister was born shortly after we moved, causing a little jealousy. Up to that point, I had been the baby for seven years, and I didn't like having to share my room. Then, three years later, my little brother was born, so I really had to share everything.

During the early years of my childhood, all appeared right in my world, from my view as I looked through my mirror. My view consisted of a beautiful mother and father whom I adored. I was undeniably a daddy's girl. I went to work with him and I felt without a doubt that my daddy loved me.

In those days, I actually had two families – our family at home and a church family with the Jehovah's Witnesses. Our church family was the center of our lives. I just felt loved within these two families. Everything seemed fine from my viewpoint as a child. Growing up as a Jehovah's Witness, I didn't know what it was to celebrate holidays, like Christmas or Easter, not even birthdays. My mom would throw parties where we could dress up and have fun but not celebrating holidays was just the norm for me. At school, it was a little different as I saw the other kids preparing for the holidays, but I had awesome teachers who let me help them while the rest of the class was doing holiday activities. I would run errands for them, like taking papers to the office or books back to the library, so I still felt accepted as part of the class.

As far as I knew, everything was good in our home. I had two loving parents and three siblings. We all appeared happy as I gazed into the mirror of my family life. That was before I turned twelve, when my mirror shattered and my world turned upside down -- the year my dad was in a bad car accident and we stopped going to church.

My father and I would often go to the restaurant where my mom worked. We would wait on her while she was closing. I usually rode with my daddy, but that particular night my mom made me ride home with her. I'm thankful she ignored the fit I probably pitched and let me be unhappy with her.

My mom and I arrived at home but my father never showed up. As we drove back looking for him, we came upon an accident scene. The red and blue lights were flashing, bouncing bright colors off the street. I was fascinated with the lights, until I saw the familiar little green Honda hatchback smashed into a light pole. I was so scared! We pulled into the median. It was dark and all the flashing lights were blinding. All I could think about was the possibility that my daddy was dead.

The lights were flashing through the mist of night air. I saw a figure walking toward us and I suddenly realized it was my father! I was so happy when he came walking up to us. Little did I know that my family mirror was about to shatter. What came next began the downward spiral of my life that would continue for a number of years.

Our church family wasn't around supporting us during this frightening time after the accident. Why weren't they here? They were like family to us. I called most of them "aunt" and "uncle" and they were always around. Now I couldn't even get them to answer my calls. I later learned they had disassociated my dad from the church for drinking. That was why we no longer were permitted to have contact with anyone.

On the heels of these traumatic events, our family underwent even more difficult changes. I remember moving to three different homes within a few short months, and we finally ended up in Orange Park, Florida. It was not much longer before my father moved out altogether. He was living with someone else, and my mom was sad all the time. My mirror was completely shattered. All I could see were cracks and missing pieces. I felt that something must be wrong with me. How could my daddy leave me? What did I do that was so wrong? Yes, it sounds as though I was thinking only of myself, but I was a child who did not understand all that was going on. I didn't see the alcoholism. I didn't see all the fighting. I didn't see all the times he came home late, or not at all. All I saw was a daddy who loved me and was now gone. All I saw was that my once-happy mother, who loved to laugh and joke with us, was now sad and cried all the time. I can only imagine the emotional turmoil going on inside her at this time. Her mirror had been shattered, as well. She had the weight of the world on her shoulders and she had to figure out how to take care of four kids on her own.

I do recall a vivid memory from this time. One evening, I remember my older sister being upset, speaking on the phone, while her best friend tried her best to persuade me to stay in the bedroom with my two younger siblings. I desperately begged her over and over to tell me what was going on. Her best friend brought us popsicles and pleaded with me to remain with the kids in the bedroom. I was upset and confused; a popsicle was the last thing I wanted. So many questions were flooding my mind. Why were strange people walking around in our house? Where was our mother? Why wouldn't anybody tell me anything? It was almost like slow motion, or a silent movie feeling. I don't remember any noise at all. My little brother and sister appeared oblivious to what was going on. They were watching TV and excited about getting popsicles. My sister and her friend were whispering, which just made me more curious. I couldn't stand it any longer -- I just had to know what was happening.

You guessed it. I didn't stay in the bedroom.

This is where the silent movie feeling came into play. There were two ways to get to my mom's room -- the hallway by the front door and through the kitchen. Everyone was in the hallway, so I went through the kitchen. When I rounded the corner to my mom's room, a paramedic stopped me. I remember catching glimpses of my mom lying on the floor. I looked at my sister and her friend for answers, but they looked as confused as I was.

Why would she be lying on the floor? She wasn't moving. Was she sick? There was a bottle of pills spilt on the floor. What was wrong? Was she hurt? Did she fall down? One of the paramedics gently drew me away, and patiently explained to me that mom was ill and promised to take good care of her. His voice was so kind, so gentle. I just remember standing and watching as they wheeled the stretcher out the door.

Over the years, as I grew into adulthood, I wondered why my siblings and I were allowed to stay at the house by ourselves that night. My older sister was only seventeen years old, yet, surprisingly, Social Services didn't get involved. I realize now that God was watching over us once again.

My grandmother showed up the next morning to stay with us. She took us to the hospital to visit my mom. I recall her telling us to make sure we told my mom how much we loved her. At the time, I don't believe I realized what had transpired. I was just scared, but only because I didn't know if my mom was going to be okay or not. I wasn't sure if she was going to be the next one to leave.

My world was turbulent with so many changes that it was difficult for me to fully understand that my family had been shattered beyond repair. Nothing looked the same. The image from my mirror looked completely different. We hadn't been back to church since the night of the accident and I didn't understand why. We were happy there, or so I thought. In my eyes, there was nothing wrong with it. I didn't see all the hurt and betrayal at the time. Being involved in the Jehovah's Witnesses was something that I'd grown up with; it was normal to me. Suddenly, our family was doing all the things I thought we shouldn't be doing, such as celebrating holidays. Up to that point in my life, I had been taught these celebrations were wrong. I still believed that, so when my mother starting allowing us to participate in these events, I felt conflicted. Looking back, I now realize it was her way of trying to help us navigate through all the difficult changes that were occurring in the life of our family. She just wanted her kids to have something fun to look forward to.

Celebrating Christmas for the first time still felt wrong. While everyone else at our house was so excited about Christmas, all I could think about was how wrong it was. For many years, I was taught by the church and at home that it was wrong. I was always the odd one out at school, but suddenly it was okay to celebrate. It was just a confusing time for me. I didn't understand all the new changes that were bombarding me all at once.

To add to the confusion and turmoil, there was an incident a couple weeks before Christmas with an adult male figure in my life. I thought I could trust him, but he only hurt me. It was unimaginable that he did it. The fact that no one believed me when I tried to describe what had happened to me left me feeling scared and alone. So there we were, supposedly a happy family celebrating Christmas, and I was miserable. I missed my life as it was, before my daddy went away. Trying to cope with all the emotions left me feeling lonely and unworthy.

At this point, my mom was working all the time to take care of us. My father was not helping and we barely saw him. I thought that if my father did not love me enough to stick around, who would? So, I started seeking attention from all the wrong people.

This was the beginning of the downward spiral of my teenage years. I was a good kid, for the most part. Although I stayed out late running around with friends and drinking, I never let things go too far with the boys. I wanted to feel loved, but did not want to give myself away in that way. I know now that is why they always left me. At the time, I figured it was because I wasn't pretty enough, or skinny enough. My self-esteem was at an all-time low and I felt unworthy to be loved. I thought if a guy paid attention to me, it meant I was loved, but love was the farthest thing from their mind. After my father left, I sought to replace the void. I wanted my mirror to be whole again. I thought the only way that would happen was if a man loved me. What I didn't know then was that there had always been a Man who loved me more than anyone else could; Jesus was right there the whole time, patiently waiting. It just took me a while to see Him standing there.

It is difficult to believe that I could still trust anyone after all I had been through. I was so desperate for the acknowledgment that I was important to anyone. I assumed the attention I received from guys would make me feel loved. So, I trusted them enough to be alone with them. Sometimes I walked away without any scars or baggage to carry, other times I didn't.

There were many nights I remember crying myself to sleep because of situations I found myself in. One particular night left me feeling the same as I did the few weeks before our first Christmas. It was a scary night for me. Here I was again with someone I thought cared for me, but all he did was hurt me. I didn't tell anyone. I couldn't bring myself to trust that anyone would believe me. Why would they? They hadn't believed me in the past. So I dealt with this incident the same way I had responded to all my other past hurts. I buried it and hid it behind the wall of protection that I was steadily building around my heart.

When I was fifteen, my father remarried. I shouldn't have been surprised. He had lived with her since he left us. My mom had boyfriends, but my father marrying someone else made me realize there was no going back. Another crack formed in my mirror. I felt I would never have a normal life again. Up to that point, I had lived in a childhood fairytale world, and I desperately wanted to believe there was still a chance for my shattered family to be put back together again. Sadly, that book was forever closed. The rug was ripped out from under me and I started falling again, feeling as though I no longer had any stable footing in my life.

With the naivety and short-sightedness of a teenager, I concluded, "If my own father didn't care how I felt, then who cares what I do or don't do?" I decided the only way I was going to find love and keep it was to give the guys what they were wanting. So I did. I thought somehow it would make things better. The boys would stay with me and I would feel loved and accepted. I found out that it definitely did not help. I was so wrong. These so-called relationships did not mend the cracks in my mirror. I only succeeded in adding more sorrow and feelings of guilt to the broken mirror of my heart. As people left me behind, I felt used and even more broken. I wanted to appear tough and brave, but in reality I was neither; I was terri-fied. I craved true love, but didn't know how to find it, so I kept searching.

"The Lord is nigh unto them that are of a broken heart; and saveth such as be of a contrite spirit." —Psalm 34:18

Chapter 3

OUR JOURNEY

I was in high school, still struggling to find my way, when Buddy showed up in my life. I didn't understand until much later that God was steadily moving in each of our lives, readying us for a future together.

Buddy also comes from a broken family, torn apart by alcoholism. As a result, he owns a shattered mirror as well. His parents divorced when he was nine years old. His mom moved him and his two sisters from Kilgore, Texas to Jacksonville, Florida, where his grandmother was at the time. He has often said that he struggled with adjusting from the country life of East Texas to the big city life in Jacksonville; it was two completely different worlds for him.

Most of his teenage years mirrored mine as a searching game, during which time he sought attention from the wrong people. His mom worked all the time, leaving him with lots of unsupervised time on his hands to find trouble. Bored with school, he eventually quit during the tenth grade. The last grade he passed was eighth and school wasn't challenging enough to suit his ADHD mind. Going to work instead of school was much more appealing to him.

Looking back, I can see how God's plan was working and weaving mine and Buddy's lives to the point where we would eventually meet. Who would have thought a girl from Hialeah, Florida and a guy from Kilgore, Texas would span that tremendous distance in miles to meet and marry? Not me, but God had plans for us.

Buddy and I met for the first time in October of 1986. To be honest, I didn't like him much. He worked with my mom at a restaurant. That particular night, a group of them came over to our house to watch movies and eat pizza. I thought he was a jerk -- cute, but still a jerk.

By November, I was working at the restaurant with my mom, but Buddy no longer worked there. One night, his family came in, and he was with them. He walked up and asked if I wanted to go to the movies with them later on. I told him he had to ask my mom. As he was walking away, I was thinking to myself, "Are you crazy?" I liked the attention, and the enticement of going out with the "bad boy" was a little hard for me to resist. My mother said I could go with him, so he told me he would be back later to pick me up. Well, he never showed up. I guess I should have stuck with my first impression of him.

A couple months went by and I was dating other guys. I just kept finding myself in situations where I felt ashamed and alone. I just wanted to be loved and couldn't find anything or anyone who could fill the emptiness within my heart. At that time, I had not found God, but thankfully He knew me, and was patiently ordering the steps of my life.

On January 24. 1987, I went into work. As I clocked in, I was surprised to see that Buddy had returned there to work. I didn't want to work with him, so I asked my manager to put me out front. I figured if I was on the front register, I could avoid eye contact with him. Of course, that was easier said than done.

Believe it or not, Buddy and I actually went out that night. Our memories differ about our first date. I thought a group of us were all going out, and when no one else but him showed up, I was convinced he had tricked me. He still claims there was no plan of coercion.

Buddy and I dated for about a year and a half. His family was affectionate and always hugging everyone, which overwhelmed me. I wasn't brought up that way, so it was a different experience for me. Buddy and I had our ups and downs. I was a naive girl who wanted to be loved and I really wanted him to be the one who would love me. I couldn't see it, but at this point he was a selfish person and it was all about him.

Buddy had been working framing houses off and on since he was sixteen. The guy he was working for at the time was also a big drug dealer, with fast cars, boats, and lots of girls. Buddy thought to himself, "Hey, I want to be like him." Well, that's what he became. I was so unsuspecting that I didn't have a clue about any of this. When I found out about it, he downplayed it and promised it would never happen again. I naively believed him and continued living in the fairytale world I preferred to exist in.

Buddy told me about a job opportunity in Texas to work with his dad and uncles at a power plant. I wasn't thrilled about him leaving, which was normal. What sixteen-year-old wants their boyfriend to move halfway across the country? I knew he needed to go because he wasn't making enough money here in Florida, but it was hard.

We talked all the time while he was gone. In the back of my mind, I was always worried it would not work out between us. We argued over the smallest things and eight months was a long time to be apart. My thoughts were confirmed when he came back to Jacksonville. Things just were not the same. I knew it for certain the day I was sitting in class at school and the girl behind me started talking about this great guy she was going out with that night. As she continued talking, it became more and more obvious she was talking about Buddy. When I confronted him, he didn't deny it. He basically told me to get over it; he was going to date her and that was that. I told him that was not going to work for me and we broke up for a few months in the fall of 1988. At the time, he was living up to his "bad boy" reputation. A couple of months went by and I tried going out with other people, but he was the one I loved, and I missed him terribly. I went back with him after he promised once again that I was the one he wanted and it was over with the other girls.

After I graduated from high school in 1989, I moved in with Buddy. We had a singlewide trailer on a piece of property. I thought things were great, but of course I did; I existed in my little bubble. My mirror still had cracks in it, but I was choosing to look passed them. I felt loved, so all was right in my world. Looking back as an adult, it was a year of craziness. We were definitely living the party lifestyle. Weekend parties with lots of drinking were the norm. Buddy was addicted to cocaine and selling it. I was oblivious to all of it even though I found drugs in our roommate's bathroom. When I flushed them down the toilet, it created quite a ruckus. Needless to say, neither the roommate nor Buddy was happy with me. Even with all the evidence right under my nose, I still didn't suspect anything. I believed everything he told me.

I remember Buddy was gone a lot. Of course I thought he was working, because that is what he told me. One evening I came home from work as usual. A few hours passed and Buddy didn't come home. I tried calling him and he wouldn't answer. The phone he had was one of those that mounted in the truck. I just kept telling myself that he wasn't in his truck. He also had a pager and I sent page after page, without a response. For three nights, I called hospitals, police stations, anyone I could think of. I was extremely worried about him and cried myself to sleep every night. I had no idea where he was or who he was with. At this point, I had convinced myself that he had to be with another girl.

After being gone for three nights, he returned home. I was sleeping at the time and he collapsed onto the couch, convinced that he was dying from a severe reaction to cocaine. He remembered going to church as a kid and hearing the gospel, so he prayed that night that if God would save him from hell and allow him to live, that he would not touch the drugs ever again. God isn't in the deal-making business, but Buddy was desperate that night. He woke up the next morning and has kept that vow.

I was thrilled when I got up the next morning and saw that he was home. Of course, he had all kinds of excuses and I believed them all. He was just thankful to be alive, but wasn't ready to share his secrets with me. In my fairy-tale world, it didn't matter if he was telling the truth or not. I was just so happy that he was home.

The happy feeling didn't last long. He told me that he was going back to Texas to go to work with his dad again. I was upset because he was leaving me once again, and I remembered what occurred the last time he left. I knew he had to go. Financially, we were in a mess. We had moved back in with his mom and had lots of bills. I just had no inkling about the real reason behind him leaving this time. He knew he had to get away if he was going to keep his vow to God. I wouldn't find out about all the details of why until about a year or so later. So, off to

Texas he went to work. I stayed behind, busy with work and I was also attending cosmetology school.

He came to Jacksonville during Christmas of 1990 to spend the holiday at home, after being gone seven long months. It was great to see him, and I was hoping that he would propose while he was home. The long distance relationship was hard on me. I just wanted to be with him and the longer we were apart the more scared I became of losing him again.

I was excited Christmas morning, hopeful that it would be the day. Well, I can't say he actually proposed, because he never even asked me to marry him. As a matter of fact, he threw the ring at me. Yes, he threw it at me. I went to his mom's house and he was walking out the door to go waterskiing. I was upset because I wanted him to open his Christmas gift from me, and I was really hoping he had a ring for me. So, he came inside the house, took an ornament off the tree, and tossed it at me. The ornament was a reindeer holding a stocking, and inside the stocking was my engagement ring. I put it on, trying to take a few minutes to admire it. I was so excited. Then, he announced that he was going waterskiing, and to come on if I was coming with him. So, that sums up my "romantic" proposal.

After Christmas, he returned to Texas. We planned to be married in June of 1991. With Buddy out of state, I was handling all the wedding plans. I would ask his opinion on things, but he never showed too much enthusiasm. That should have been my first clue that something was up.

All I could focus on was getting married and living happily ever after. My mirror was on the mend, or so I thought.

Five weeks prior to the wedding, I had gotten all of the invitations addressed and ready to mail. I was getting so excited about the wedding. All the details were coming together and I was finally going to be married. I felt life couldn't get any better. Buddy called the night before I was going to the post office to mail out the invitations. I was telling him all about the plans. He stopped me and told me he didn't want to get married. I was stunned and may have giggled thinking he must have been joking. When he said it again, I realized he was serious. I was beyond devastated. When I asked him why, he just kept telling me he wasn't ready. When I hung up the phone, I just remember crying so hard that my nose bled. My mom hugged me, trying to comfort me but there was nothing anyone could say at that time. I vividly remember her white t-shirt stained red from my nosebleed. My fairytale was coming apart. My somewhat-mended mirror had cracked once again.

It was a difficult time for me. Everyone was asking me why we weren't getting married, and I had no answers. I didn't even understand it myself. He was in Texas and didn't have to deal with any of the fallout. I couldn't even force myself to go back to the dress shop to retrieve my senior prom dress I was having redone for the wedding. I think about it often, but have no idea what ever became of the dress.

So you are probably thinking, "Are you done with him now, you crazy girl?" No, I wasn't.

Buddy returned home the week we were supposed to get married because his sister was graduating from high school. The original plan was for him to come home for the graduation, we were going to get married, and I was going to fly back with him to Texas. I had already purchased my plane ticket. Back in those days, it was cheaper to buy a round-trip ticket and not use the return flight. So, I had a round-trip ticket to Texas. I don't remember if Buddy asked me to go back with him or not. Maybe I thought somehow I could get him to change his mind about getting married. However, after our week together in Texas ended, he brought me back to the airport and said to me, "You go home and live your life. I will live mine and if our paths cross and we can make it work, we will." I was crushed watching him walk away and feeling as though I had wasted five years of my life. I got on the plane, took off my engagement ring, and threw it in my purse. The man sitting beside me just looked at me. I said, "Don't ask." It was a long quiet plane ride back to Jacksonville.

Well, I went home and did exactly what Buddy said for me to do. I starting going out with other people. Although he had told me to go home and live my life, he still called the same time every week. I purposely stayed away from the house whenever he called. A month went by without me talking to him. One day, while I was checking the mail, there was a card from him. I almost fell over in shock and disbelief. He hardly ever wrote, and it was totally unexpected that he actually went to the store and picked out a card, especially for me. I was shocked. I read it and thought for a split second that I should be home when he called the next time. I decided that just one card was not going to do it and continued avoiding his calls. Then the letters started coming. I like to call it the "begging and pleading." We talked a couple of times on the phone, but I was sort of seeing someone else and I did not know if I wanted to take another chance and get hurt again. Finally, in September of 1991, he convinced me to come out to Texas. He wanted me to give him two weeks - if I wasn't happy in two weeks, I could go home. So, I loaded up my car with all of my stuff and a one hundred pound bulldog and drove from Jacksonville to San Antonio, Texas. It was my first time to really be off on my own.

Two weeks went by, and I decided to stay. During that time, he told me everything about the drugs and how involved he was in them. Not only was he using, but he was also dealing. I was shocked. He told me this was the real reason behind him leaving again to go back to Texas, and then he went into detail about the night he thought he was dying from the effects of cocaine. He knew that to stay clean, he had to get away from those people who were involved in drugs and change his scenery.

I know you are probably thinking, "She was so naïve." You're right, I was. I had never experimented with drugs; they scared me. I was happy and felt loved by him, so I could not see any of the bad aspects. My mind just blocked out the bad, and I believed every excuse and every promise. He did a really good job of hiding it. Looking back, I can see all the warning signs that I didn't see then. I guess that's why they say hindsight is 20/20. I now believe it was just God's way of keeping me around. I don't know if I would've stuck around had I known everything. Drugs were scary to me, and I probably would've run away in the opposite direction. Unbeknownst to me, God was using my "not knowing" to help keep me in Buddy's life.

I thought things were going well. I'd been with Buddy in Texas for ten months. No, he didn't ask me to marry him, but he did ask me to start wearing my engagement ring again. We had talked about marriage and actually planned one date that didn't work out. I have to admit that I changed my mind at that time, not because I didn't love him or want to marry him, but the timing just didn't work out.

One afternoon, we were riding in the truck. Out of the blue he said that I should go back to Florida. He didn't think things were going to work out for us. I was completely numb. I didn't get emotional over it. Maybe I was in shock, or denial. I do remember sitting there, looking out the window and knowing that I had heard him, but I wished I hadn't. I asked him if he was sure and he said yes. I didn't know what to do or say in response. Just when I thought that our relationship had gained traction, and a bright future for us was within sight, everything shattered once again. I was beginning to wonder if I would ever have the stable, loving relationship I craved.

He was working the night shift, so I packed my car and went over to spend the night with a couple that we knew. I told them about the conversation with Buddy and that the next day I would be heading back home to Florida for good. When I was getting ready to head out the next morning, the husband, a co-worker of Buddy's, told me I needed to go see Buddy before I left. I argued with him for a few minutes and finally decided I would go and say goodbye.

I remember walking into our trailer and he was already in bed. I told him I was heading out. I don't exactly remember what all was said, but he told me that our friend had spoken to him and knocked some sense into him and he wanted me to stay. I told him that it had to be his final decision, and I wasn't unpacking my car, he could. I had no intention of going through this turmoil again.

At the end of July 1992, a group of us who traveled together to different jobs all headed to Florida for a job in Okeechobee. When we got there, we called Buddy's mom and said to get everything ready—we would be home in two weeks to get married. So, on August 22, 1992, we finally got married; "third time is the charm," they say.

We lived in Okeechobee until the beginning of 1994, and then we moved to Orlando for another job. Church and God were still the furthest thing from our minds. We went a few times to various churches, but they were always preaching on tithing or commitment. Buddy said he wouldn't "give his hard-earned money so that a preacher could buy a new car." We had a lot to learn, but God was being patient with us.

Our daughter, Julie, was born in August 1994. We were living in Orlando in a thirty-foot travel trailer. Buddy's job was starting to wind down. The company he was working for wanted him to go back to Texas, but we really didn't want to go back. We heard about a job over in Mulberry, which was on the southwest side of Orlando. We decided to visit the area, hoping that it might be a good fit for our growing family.

We started looking for a place to live over there and promptly got lost. Looking back, I realize now that by getting literally lost, we eventually found God.

The result of us getting lost was that we found a community named Bay Lake, a small-unincorporated area outside Groveland. It was nice and a quiet place out in the country. In the beginning of 1995, we bought ten acres of land there and made our home in a doublewide trailer, while Buddy drove to and from his job in Mulberry. A pretty little church was located right across the road from us, but our focus was more on the view of the lake, so at first we didn't take much notice of the church. God was working; we just didn't know it at the time.

The job ended in Mulberry, and the company still wanted him to go back to Texas. I told him he should take his 401K money and start building houses again. So, he did. Everything was good, until he fell twenty-eight feet off a roof and broke his foot. After being laid up for a few weeks, he started doing small jobs around the area, and then went to North Carolina to work on a power plant for a few weeks. I was pregnant with our son, Luke, so Buddy decided he needed to find something around home. He was working for a company building houses as a superintendent, but was completely miserable. He hated the job.

In August 1997, he was invited to Bay Lake Missionary Baptist Church for homecoming services. This was the church across the street from us to which we hadn't been paying any attention. I told him he could go if he wanted, but I was not going. Because of my childhood experiences with the Jehovah's Witnesses, I didn't want to have anything to do with any church whatsoever, plus I was eight months pregnant. So, he and Julie went.

This is how he describes his first visit to that church: "I thought the preacher must have been reading my mail, talking to my friends, and listening to my conversations, because he seemed to know everything I was thinking." It broke him that day and he knew that God had saved him the night he was lying on the couch, dealing with the effects of cocaine, and thinking he was dying. Buddy realized that he hadn't been living for God and needed to start.

The ladies of the church insisted Buddy go home and bring me back for lunch. They celebrate an annual homecoming with services, lunch on the grounds, and an afternoon sing. Homecoming is held during the third week of

August in Central Florida. It was hot and I was pregnant, so you can probably imagine that I wasn't exactly enthusiastic when Buddy came home and told me about the invitation. He said, "Please don't make me look like a fool. Just come back for lunch." I went, but wanted to come home right after lunch. I was miserable; not only because I was hot, but I was also having an uncomfortable feeling, which I later realized was due to my being under conviction from the Holy Spirit. That is not a comfortable feeling when you are trying to hide or run from it.

Buddy had met a guy that wanted to partner with him and start a framing business. It sounded too good to be true and he didn't call him back until a few days after homecoming. He got up that morning for work, already mad and frustrated with his job. On August 25th, just nine days before Luke was born, he told me he was quitting his job and going to work with this guy. I won't lie -- I was a little freaked out. I knew he would take care of us, but I was nine months pregnant.

Buddy tells the story of how the church ladies brought meals and tried to show their love to us after Luke was born. I don't remember it quite the way he does, but I didn't want to have anything to do with organized religion. From my past experience, all I remembered was pain associated with church. God's people did not love me before, so I wasn't anxious to allow any more church people into my life.

I had done a lot of reading on the Jehovah's Witnesses and how they began, as well as other books on religion. I didn't agree with the beliefs of the Jehovah's Witnesses, but truthfully I didn't know exactly what, or who, to believe. There was a void in my spiritual life, and I kept searching for something to fill it.

Buddy and Julie had been attending the Sunday morning service at Bay Lake Baptist Church for a while. I was still hesitant, too scared to let my guard down, but finally started attending. They had a new pastor and I liked listening to him. He really held our attention, and didn't bash all the other religions. I remember him saying one time that being Baptist was like wearing a certain military uniform. It just signified what you claim to believe in. He also said there would be lots of people in heaven who were not Baptist, because the only way to heaven was through a personal relationship with Jesus, so the door to heaven was open to anyone who believed that Jesus died on the cross for their sins and rose again, returning to heaven. That made sense to me. The pastor and his wife came over to our house a few times to discuss my concerns and I finally decided it was right for me. So Buddy and I joined the church.

"For God so loved the world, that he gave his only begotten Son, that whosoever believeth in him should not perish, but have everlasting life." —John 3:16

Chapter 4

OUR ROLLER COASTER RIDE

I had gotten saved and Buddy was re-dedicating his life to the Lord. Now would be the time in our lives that everything would be perfect, right? Nope, sorry. This is a big misconception of newly saved individuals. Reality is, this is the time that the devil likes to interfere, stoking the fire and attacking from all angles. The next season of our lives found us experiencing many personal and business struggles. Our faith wavered, but God was faithful through all of the challenges.

Buddy was completely focused on getting the company going, and I believe the devil was completely focused on tearing me apart with self-doubt. During this time, I was fragile. If someone was upset or mad, I instantly assumed I'd done something wrong, or it was somehow my fault whenever any problems occurred. I believed everyone was looking at me and my life thinking how perfect it was for us, so I had to keep up the appearance that we were leading a perfect life. Internally, I felt as though I was in the midst of cracking. The bitter, miserable person on the inside was trying to come out. There was a spiritual tug of war going on within me. I believe most days the devil was winning.

Actually, I believe we all look at the lives of others and think everything is perfect for them, but we have no idea of what they are dealing with behind their closed doors. I think if we all cast our problems into a pile and saw everyone else's difficulties, we'd gratefully grab ours back.

Over the years, I have fought depression and contemplated suicide. I have tried to drown my pain with alcohol. Although I was saved, I was still searching to find love, to find someone -- or something -- to make me feel safe and secure. It took me awhile to learn that I would not find freedom from doubt, anxiety, or worry through anything the world has to offer; only Jesus offers the unbreakable promise to love and accept us just as we are. God's acceptance of me as His child -- His daughter -- was all I needed to feel complete. It is all anyone needs but you must be willing to accept it. I had accepted the gift of salvation, but I hadn't learned how to accept all His promises. Some people have the misconception that once you are saved, you are instantly happy forever. That just isn't the case. We need to learn how to seek joy instead of happiness.

There is a difference between joy and happiness. Happiness is just feelings or emotions based on your situation. You can be really happy one moment and stub your toe and not be so happy the next. Joy should be inside us all the time, once we accept Christ as our Savior. True joy is found by placing Jesus first, others second, and yourself last. A verse that convicts me whenever I try to rely upon my human reason and logic is Isaiah 55:8: "'For my thoughts are not your thoughts, neither are your ways my ways,' saith the Lord." How I would handle a situation is not always the way God ultimately handles it, but I had to experience Him at work many times in our lives to learn reliance upon Him, which breathed true certainty into my once uncertain life.

All through the years growing up, I learned to hide my true feelings behind a wall that I created within myself to protect me from hurt. Lowering the wall only resulted in my being vulnerable to attacks, so I kept a barrier between others and myself. Each time I got hurt, another row of blocks added to my wall. I didn't want to let anyone in because I assumed they were just going to leave me. As a mean of self-defense, I intentionally pushed people away so that I wouldn't get hurt when they left. In my mind, I was convinced they would leave me. I even went as far as doing things to push Buddy away, hoping he would stay distant so that when he eventually left, it would not be as painful. I'd seen failed marriages and relationships happening within the lives of my friends and family, so I fully expected that I would ultimately be a single mom raising my kids on my own, just like my mom.

I was also dealing with several health issues during this time – anxiety, high blood pressure, and anemia. I underwent every possible medical test, but no one could find anything that could medically explain the source for my health problems. I even had a doctor tell me that I was a thirty-year-old housewife with nothing to be stressed over. Needless to say, I did not see him again. I was just miserable, but I maintained a front of appearing to have everything under control. There were few people who knew what was going on with me, which only increased my feelings of loneliness and isolation.

Sometimes we become completely overwhelmed with life. We focus on all the cracks and missing pieces of our mirror instead of placing our faith in God. When we learn to cast all our burdens on Christ, those large cracks in the mirror appear to close up a little, because nothing is impossible if we keep our eyes on the Cross. Some of us are just more hardheaded and stubborn and it takes a while to learn how to cast those burdens and leave them, once and for all, at the Cross, without taking them up again. I am encouraged by 1 Peter 5:7: "Cast all your care upon him, for he careth for you." This verse of only eleven words is powerful in everlasting truth, and I've come to rely upon it many times whenever I am tempted to worry and carry all my burdens by myself.

My breaking point finally came when I began contemplating suicide. I remember thinking if I was gone from this earth, everything would be better. I didn't think about the sorrow and hurt it would cause for those I loved, and who loved me. I just wanted the pain to stop. I had made a series of bad decisions and felt I was coming apart at the seams. Fear kept me from sharing everything going on in my head. Buddy knew something was wrong with me. He told me I had to get some help. I finally reached out to a therapist. She was a wonderful Christian lady who helped me so much. I went in to her office thinking I was going to get sympathy and that I could blame everything on my past. She quickly informed me that I was responsible for all my actions as an adult, no matter what I had dealt with as a child. So we started the long process of tearing down walls. Allowing people into my comfort zone was a scary process. Getting to the point of understanding that Buddy was not going anywhere was the toughest obstacle to overcome. He had told me so many times, but in my mind I couldn't understand why he would want to stay. Why would he want to? Looking through my mirror, I felt there was nothing lovable about me.

Today, I know in my heart that he loves me and wants me, but my head always casts doubt and uncertainty. I know these thoughts are caused by the devil, seeking to undermine me. I am definitely a work in progress. I'm learning to have God help me to erase the negative garbage that the devil puts in my head. I have thirty plus years of it swirling around in there, telling me I am unworthy and unlovable and Satan loves to use it against me.

The self-doubt still creeps in often. I catch myself thinking about the "what if's" and if I am good enough. However, God comforts my thoughts, reminding me that I am one of His. No, I was not good enough, but with Jesus as my Savior, I am redeemed. That does not make me perfect -- far from it. However, I know that no matter what I do or think, God loves me and He will never leave me nor forsake me. I didn't know any of this growing up. How could God love me? My earthly father made choices that made me feel unloved. What I thought were God's people had abandoned us. How could God love me? When my head begins throwing doubts and troubling my mind, I lean on Psalm 94:18-19:

"When I said, 'My foot slippeth,' thy mercy, O Lord, held me up. In the multitude of my thoughts within me thy comforts delight my soul."

During my time of seeing the therapist, we began trying to deal with my physical health issues as well as mental issues. I started doing lots of research on my own, trying all the natural remedies to feel better physically. I am a big advocate of natural herbal remedies. I am not opposed to going to the doctor, but that usually is not my first line of defense. I did learn during all my testing that I have pernicious anemia. My body cannot break down B-12 because I am missing an intrinsic factor in my gastric secretions. So, I am required to have B-12 shots or sublingual pills. I opted for the pill because I hate needles. I believe that there were other factors contributing to all my issues, but once my B-12 levels were under control, I started feeling better.

Little did I know that God was leading me to the shop where I started buying my herbs. There, I met a wonderful friend. She has helped me navigate through this journey I have been on. She was a shoulder to cry on and the cheerleader that kept me moving forward. I felt safe confiding in her because she was not inside my normal circle of friends. I was reserved about sharing my feelings with people I spent a lot of time with. In my mind, I was worried they would look at me differently. We all need that one person we feel safe sharing things with. So, going to the shop and sharing was my safe haven. Our relationship today is one I truly cherish. I know I can count on her to make me share my feelings and not hide behind my wall.

To feel better mentally, I continued seeing the therapist and enrolled in a journaling class. This began my journey in dealing with all the issues from my past. I had to start forgiving, which was difficult. The most difficult part was first forgiving myself. Everyone makes choices in life, and the fallout affects everyone around them. I had done things that hurt people close to me. I had to forgive myself and ask them for forgiveness, as well. We can apologize, but sometimes the scars remain.

Just like when we accept Jesus, we are forgiven, but that doesn't erase any of the bad consequences from our past. We still have to deal with those. People should see a difference in us, but sometimes they cannot forgive as easily as God does. I wish we could, but our fleshly side gets involved. The world teaches us to seek revenge, but God requires that we forgive. No, it isn't easy, and just because we forgive someone doesn't mean we reconcile with him or her. Reconciliation is two-sided and sometimes it doesn't happen. Sometimes we have to forgive and move on so we don't continue to be hurt.

I have forgiven my father for the harm he caused our family with years of drinking and selfishness, but I do not have a relationship with him. It still hurts that I have not spoken to him in many years. I think about all the things he has missed. He has beautiful grandchildren with whom he doesn't have a relationship. He wasn't sitting on the front row at my daughter's wedding. It's sad that he has missed out on so much. All I can do is to continue to pray for him.

I have learned that God allows difficult circumstances to come into our lives so we can grow closer to Him. He will calm our storms. He will bring peace out of the desolation.

"Come, behold the works of the Lord, what desolations he hath made in the earth. He maketh wars to cease unto the end of the earth; he breaketh the bow, and cutteth the spear in sunder; he burneth the chariot in the fire. Be still, and know that I am

God: I will be exalted among the heathen, I will be exalted in the earth."—Psalm 46:8-10

As time wore on, Buddy was still focused with work. The business was having its struggles. He and his partner were unequally yoked. I believe that particular verse in the Bible applies to business relationships, as well, which tells us: "Be ye not unequally yoked together with unbelievers: for what fellowship hath righteousness with unrighteousness? And what communion hath light with darkness?" (2 Corinthians 6:14)

After seven years of dealing with the incompatibility and struggles, the partner said he wanted out. Buddy was relieved to finally be on his own, but shortly realized the company was bankrupt and in trouble. Buddy said he knew nothing about running a business—he just knew how to build a house. It was a difficult undertaking to start over. His ex-partner was always focused on making the company the biggest. Buddy's philosophy was to be the best. So he started rebuilding the company by letting go of all but one of his customers and focused on doing the best job he could for them. A few months into the rebuilding, it was time to pay the final payment to the ex-partner. Buddy had exhausted every measure to raise the money. We just didn't have it. He finally prayed and asked the Lord, "If this is what I am supposed to be doing then, Lord, please show me." Well, the Lord did.

Every February we received a rebate check from the insurance company. Well, this was December and miraculously, the check came early and was just the right amount we needed to buy out the former business partner. Buddy said, "Okay, Lord, here we go." He said that the only business partner he needed or wanted from then on was the Lord.

During all the struggles of the business, we were also dealing with Buddy having a severe unknown medical condition. There were times when he was in so much pain that he would have to pull his truck over to the side of the road. The sharp, electric-shock stabs of pain running from his ear to his jaw did not last long, but it stopped him in his tracks and made him close his eyes tightly. He would rub the side of his face even though he knew it wouldn't help relieve the pain. It would come and go, getting worse each time. Over the course of several years, he went to many doctors. The dentist extracted some teeth and repaired others, however, the pain continued. An ENT doctor diagnosed him with Temporomandibular Joint Dysfunction (TMJ). Buddy went through all the procedures for that diagnosis. Two years later, still in pain, he assumed he would just have to learn to live with it.

I prayed every day that God would send us the answer. It is always tough to watch your spouse or kids suffer and not be able to do anything about it. It's one of our hardest jobs as a wife or mother.

One day, I went to see a new dentist and told her about Buddy. The dentist was intrigued and wanted to meet with him. At first, Buddy refused, but finally agreed. The dentist examined Buddy and explained the different conditions she had been researching. She referred him to a facial-pain specialist. He had struggled with the pain for so long, he really didn't believe it could be fixed, so he waited several months until a week of severe pain and sleepless nights convinced him that it was time to see the specialist. As fellow hunters, they hit it off immediately. Within ten minutes of discussing hunts and his pain, the specialist provided the diagnosis, "It's Trigeminal Neuralgia." Those words sounded huge when first pronounced to us. This disorder is characterized by episodes of intense facial pain that can last anywhere from a few seconds to several minutes or hours. The cause is due to the cerebellum artery lying on the nerve, which wears the lining down, thereby leaving an exposed nerve. Buddy's pain ran the length from his ear to his jaw. It is also known as the "suicide disease," because it results in the most excruciating pain known to man, and often goes undiagnosed. It's unusual for someone in his or her mid-thirties to have such a severe case, so that can sometimes mean a tumor is causing the pain. The doctor wanted to run more tests.

We were feeling a measure of relief that someone had finally put a name on it, but still frightened that he could possibly have a brain tumor. The next few weeks were an intense period of time, as he underwent tests and anxiously awaited results. The specialist finally called with great news -- there was no tumor. We were relieved. The medical issue was still there to deal with, but we were thankful that prayers had been answered and he didn't have a brain tumor.

The prescribed medication affected Buddy's short-term memory, as well as his temper. He became hard to live with. We all walked around on eggshells hoping to not set off the fuse. It was a whole new challenge for me to navigate through his moods and keep the kids focused on other things. The wedding vow of "in sickness and health" became a reality. I finally told him that he had to try something different, because the medication did not completely control the pain and our family was miserable.

Since the medication was not working, the specialist suggested a surgery known as Microvascular Decompression, which was another mouthful of medical syllables for us to learn to pronounce. The procedure consisted of going in behind the ear and separating the nerve and artery, and then wrapping Teflon gauze around the nerve to protect it, thereby halting the pain. According to the specialist, the best surgeon for this particular treatment was located in Pittsburgh, Pennsylvania. We decided if Buddy required brain surgery, then we were going to the best. We flew to Pittsburgh to meet with the surgeons and had the surgery scheduled for June 2006. They wanted to do it that week, but Buddy told them he wanted to go turkey hunting one more time "just in case they messed him up, leaving him unable to hunt again."

Interestingly enough, when June rolled around, the pain had gone away. He decided not to have the surgery. When we called the medical team in Pennsylvania, they strongly advised him to go ahead and have the procedure done. They told him the pain would eventually return, and when it did, it would be even worse. Buddy still chose to wait it out. He thought maybe God had healed him, and he wasn't undergoing brain surgery if he didn't need it.

Unfortunately, the doctors were right. A year later, the pain was so intense that he could hardly sleep or eat. We called Pennsylvania again, and they said to come on in. Well, Buddy had some hunting trips planned. You guessed it -- he just had to go on those hunts just in case they messed him up. He later said that he wished he had the surgery instead. He was miserable with pain and was barely able to hunt.

January 2008 found us freezing in Pittsburgh – Buddy was finally undergoing surgery. He said he went to sleep hurting, woke up pain-free, and is still pain-free today. I was relieved when he woke up after the four hour procedure and remembered me. My greatest fear was that he would not recognize me when he woke up from surgery.

I was beginning to see light at the end of the tunnel. I really felt that God had answered our prayers. Buddy's pain was gone and we felt as if we were on the right track.

I thought the roller coaster was coming to a stop, when out of nowhere, it shot off in another direction.

The economic downturn in 2008 caused a mess in the housing market. It meant we had to make some major adjustments in our life. Money became tight with all extra going back into the company to keep it going. We had cut our budget everywhere we thought we could, including letting our ranch workers go. Doing so meant we had to move to the ranch to manage things ourselves, but God was still holding everything together. It was a big adjustment for everyone. We left our home in Bay Lake that we had built and although the ranch was only seventeen miles away from there, the kids thought it might as well have been Alaska.

By April of 2011, things were still not good, financially. I could sense Buddy's stress, which meant things were still not good at work. It was that time of year when we would spend a week at the fairgrounds for our county fair. Our kids showed animals for FFA. There was a campground near the fair, and we would bring our camper. Buddy drove back and forth to work. One night, he came in after work and I could just read the distress upon him. He was quiet, but I knew something was up. The next morning he had not left for work when I got up, which was highly unusual. I asked him what he was doing. He said, "I'm not going to work. I am done."

I didn't know what that meant, so I numbly sat and asked him to help me understand. He explained that all of his leases for the business were due the following month, and there was not enough money to pay the bills, so the only conclusion he could draw was that we were done. I said, "Okay, here we go again, but I support whatever decision you make and I trust you to take care of us."

I sounded courageous, but my heart was breaking for him. Buddy actually quit. He said that maybe God had other plans for him. He was completely miserable. He wanted to trust God, but letting go of everything that he had worked for was like admitting that he had failed. Buddy has been driven by the fear of failure ever since he dropped out of school. His grandfather had written him a letter and told him he would be a bum and mooch the rest of his life. Once again, he was haunted by his grandfather's prediction, and it hurt him deeply.

About an hour later, as he was leaving, I asked where was he going. He said he had to go the office and figure out how to shut everything down. It was so hard to watch him look so defeated. I know he had been up all night pouring his heart out to God.

Not long after he left, he called me crying. He had called the office on his way in and was asking about some money he knew was owed to him. The accounts receivable clerk asked if he'd been praying. He told her that he'd been praying all night. She said that God must have heard his prayers because she had just received an email from one of the builders. The check they were sending that week was more than Buddy expected. It was more than we needed! Then, he received another phone call regarding a new building to lease that required a lower monthly payment. God was showing up -- big time.

Just days later, God also worked out a situation with our ranch payment so that we could also keep the ranch. God was blessing us all around, telling Buddy that all He wanted was his faith in Him, and that He would do the rest. Matthew 17:20 says:

And Jesus said unto them, "Because of your unbelief: for verily I say unto you, 'If ye have faith as a grain of mustard seed, ye shall say unto this mountain, Remove hence to yonder place;' and it shall remove; and nothing shall be impossible unto you."

This became the verse that kept Buddy going. He finally read and noticed the last part that said, "nothing shall be impossible unto you." God never lets us down. He sometimes makes us wait longer than we would like, but He always takes care of us.

Buddy truly has a heart for God. I believe he does all he can to be a witness for God and how He can bless us when we allow Him to. Every time someone asks how his business keeps growing, he has the opportunity to share his testimony about how great our God is.

Who would've thought today he'd be running multiple companies with hundreds of employees? Again, only God knew what would eventually occur in our lives. Buddy always says he is not good enough or smart enough to be where he is today, so it must be God who is ultimately responsible for making things happen. It has not been an easy road for Buddy, but he craves challenges. He enjoys creating things, battling a challenge, and winning.

He describes his residential home shell contracting organization as a "mom and pop shop," but with hundreds of employees, most people wouldn't describe it that way. It has grown substantially over the years, and by the grace of God, survived one of the most difficult economic downturns in the history of residential home building. In many ways, the business also mirrors what we, as parents, observe in raising children. When we blink, the kids have suddenly grown up. The same has been true with the business. We never dreamt that it would grow the way it has, but God has directed the growth as He continually propels us forward, directing our paths along the way.

"The effectual fervent prayer of a righteous man availeth much."–James 5:16

So, the business was doing well once again. Therefore, our personal life must also be doing well, or so we thought.

Through the years, Buddy and I drifted parallel down the same path. He at work and me at home, thinking all was good between us, but in reality, things were not going well between us at all. We had no idea what the other person was thinking or feeling. He would come home and be uncomfortable because I had everything running smoothly and the kids were involved in doing their own activities. I felt the same way about his work. I had no clue what he actually did. Yes, he took care of us and I felt that we were doing okay. I just thought that we were doing all the right things with me keeping everything going at home and him working to support the family. However, doing "okay" is not good enough. God wants better things for us. Had we continued drifting down that path parallel to each other, without doing things together as a team, by the time the kids grew up and left home, Buddy and I would have been to the point where we no longer knew each other. I think a lot of married couples are living this very same way, and when the kids leave, they divorce. I know divorce happens sometimes, but that is not God's plan. When Buddy came home one night and expressed his concern, we decided we were going to fight to fix our marriage.

He sat down at the table and said we have to talk. I had no idea what was going on. Of course, all the negative garbage in my head started swirling. I could feel the fear sweeping in around me like fog. Buddy looked at me and said, "I love you, but I don't know you." Wow, I was shell-shocked. Hadn't we been doing all the right things? We had been together twenty plus years. How could he not know me? My mind instantly went to the thought, "he is going to leave me. I am going to be alone."

It was a hard pill to swallow that night. Sitting across the table from each other, I was scared and could almost hear the sound of another crack forming in my mirror. I could feel all my old insecurities creeping back to the surface, but we chose to not give up. We both committed ourselves to working to save our relationship. We decided to love on purpose. After nearly twenty-five years together, we had to learn about each other all over again, starting almost anew by figuring out what each of us likes and doesn't like. We had to learn how to listen to each other and decide to put each other first.

We started making more time for each other. I always thought he was too busy and I didn't want to bother him. It turns out that he wanted me to get in his way and interrupt him. So, I started sending random text messages throughout the day: "I love you", "Thinking of you", or a smiley face. Just something to let him know he was on my mind. I also started reading a devotional every night about loving your spouse. I would send Buddy an email with the scripture and what it was about. Being the early bird that he is, he started looking forward to his morning emails. I still try to do this every night. It just gives us an opportunity to have more communication with each other. We discuss them throughout the day sometimes. It was also a way to bring God in to help us grow closer to one another. The only way to experience a close, loving relationship is to follow the best example of love: God. The closer you get to God, the more love you can give to others.

It was not an easy task. It was hard. Just like I tell my kids, marriage is not all rose petals and candlelight dinners. It is hard work and challenging at times. You must be prepared to remain committed to your vows and do whatever it takes to make it work. It is real easy to give up, but you miss out on so many blessings from God when you take the easy road. Deciding to fight is so much harder, but much more rewarding.

We have learned recently that the only way for a marriage to survive is through unconditional love, forgiveness, and communication. Satan has a harder time getting in the middle of, and separating, a couple if these three things exist. These things require complete honesty, even when it hurts. You have to be accountable to each other.

Unconditional love is a must. You have to be willing to love your spouse at all times, even if you don't like them on some days. It can be a struggle. This is a sacrificial and selfless love. We must be willing to give up our wants and desires and be a servant. Just think about how God loved us even before we loved Him. Showing love to someone is the best way to display God's love to him or her.

Forgiveness is also an absolute must in a marriage. We have to be willing to forgive each other. We are not perfect and we will mess up. I know there are some circumstances that will be more challenging to forgive. We must be willing. God will help mend any failure if we let Him. When we come through it, we will be stronger because of it.

Communication is vital in a healthy marriage. We have to be willing to share our dreams and desires with our spouse. If you expect them to just read your mind, you are going to be disappointed. We are asking for the impossible if we expect them to fulfill our unexpressed desires, and disappointment is inevitable. Once our spouse shares their desires and dreams with us, we have to be willing to do our best to honor them. If we don't, someone else will. I know that sounds harsh, but none of us are perfect. If we don't feel loved by our husband and another man pays attention to us, we notice. Conversely, if our husbands don't feel respect from us, when someone else gives them that attention, they notice. That is human nature. Just like kids who seek attention, they will find it in the right or wrong people; adults are no different.

After that difficult season in our marriage, and working hard in drawing back together, I can say today that I am more in love with my husband than ever before.

We were recently able to fulfill one of my dreams by purchasing a get-away home in the Florida Keys. We enjoy being on the water and the peace and quiet. It gives us an opportunity to escape the daily grind and reconnect with one another. It has been a fabulous investment, not only the real estate side of it, but most importantly it was an investment in our marriage. Making time for one another is crucial to any relationship.

Buddy and I find ourselves talking a lot about the past, where we came from, and where we are now. It is really unbelievable. It has been quite a roller coaster ride, but I cannot imagine being on it with anyone else. I would have to say that we are closer now than the day we got married. We are not perfect, but we are perfect for each other. God has definitely blessed us in a mighty way. It is just amazing where our lives are today. I never imagined it would be so adventurous. I know there will be more twists and turns on our ride, because we haven't gotten off yet. I know God is right there to guide and protect us as long as we follow Him.

"He healeth the broken in heart, and bindeth up their wounds."–Psalm 147:3:

Chapter 5

LEAVING A LEGACY

So I have described some of the major loops of our roller coaster. Those were some difficult times. You know that feeling you get when the ride is slowing down to stop? You look around and check to make sure everything is still intact. Well, we survived intact, but only by the grace of God. It wasn't all big, scary loops. Sometimes, we coasted along on the slow sections. There were always daily struggles along the way.

I would say the most challenging of those daily struggles was raising kids, but not because they were bad. With both of us coming from broken homes, we wanted better for our kids. I think all parents feel that way. Most of the time, people will either follow in the footsteps of their parents or do the opposite. When we become adults, we have to take responsibility for our own actions. We are the only ones that will answer to God for our actions. Sometimes, we are blessed with great examples to follow, other times we are not. Blaming our parents, or anyone else, will not do us any good. All we can do is learn from the people in our lives and try to do better. We can't always see what our parents may have been dealing with at the time. They made decisions based on their feelings. Yes, sometimes they made selfish decisions, but sometimes they were just in survival mode themselves.

Although we saw and experienced what alcoholism did to our families, we still drank. I guess we thought we would be different. That, by some chance, we wouldn't end up just like them somewhere down the road. When I got pregnant with Julie, Buddy made the decision that he wouldn't drink since I couldn't. After Julie was born, he decided he did not need it anymore. If he lasted nine months, then obviously he didn't need it. He hasn't had a drop of alcohol since December of 1993. I wish I could say the same for me.

I drank off and on from the time I was fourteen years old. I used it as an excuse to drown my pain for many years. By the time both kids were born, I would probably have classified myself as a social drinker. I would have an occasional drink when we went out. However, with two young kids and being a one-income household, we didn't go out often.

When I was dealing with all my health issues, a doctor recommended I drink a glass of red wine with dinner. Well, that might work for those who don't have an addictive nature, but it didn't work for me. One with dinner became one while making dinner, then to one after dinner. Before

I knew it, I was a regular customer at the local winery buying cases at a time. I was completely miserable while I tried to hide it from everyone. I had every excuse you could think of. I finally realized that I wasn't doing myself any good. Whatever health benefits I was supposed to gain were going down the tubes, because I was becoming an alcoholic. The alcohol was not helping; it was only leaving me feeling more lost. Eventually, it was going to tear my family apart.

It always starts out so small and innocent. Before long, you are in so deep that it is hard to find your way out. It is one of Satan's biggest tools. I'm thankful my children were young and don't remember their mom in that way. It's been several years since I made the decision to not drink. It hasn't been easy and it's an area of my life that I have to remain guarded about.

"Wine is a mocker, strong drink is raging: and whosoever is deceived thereby is not wise." – Proverbs 20:1

Raising kids made us rethink a lot of things in our life. They became the focus and priority. We were not the perfect parents. It's impossible to be the perfect parent. It isn't going to happen; we aren't perfect people. However, if we try to follow God's leadership and raise them according to the Bible, we have a good start.

I have always placed a lot of attention on protecting my kids ("momma bear syndrome" is how I refer to it). I never wanted my kids to feel like they weren't important to me. I have tried to be supportive of them at all times. Even when they have made mistakes, I tried to be there with open arms. My kids make me want to be a better person. I strive to grow into a better person so that I can be an example to them. They give me strength to continue going forward.

"And thou shalt love the Lord thy God with all thine heart, and with all thy soul, and with all thy might. And these words, which I command thee this day, shall be in thine heart: And thou shalt teach them diligently unto thy children, and shalt talk of them when thou sittest in thine house, and when thou walkest by the way, and when thou liest down, and when thou risest up."–Deuteronomy 6:5-7

It feels like just yesterday that they were born. I remember both days so clearly. Now, Julie is a married woman living across the country from me. Luke is almost grown and will be leaving next. How did that happen? "Don't blink" is all I can say. Kids grow up fast. I remember thinking being a parent of a teenager stinks. Because we make the rules, kids often think of us as the "bad guys". I didn't know if we would survive the teenage years, but we all did.

Growing up in a small town, the kids didn't have a chance to get away with anything. Everyone knew who they were and what they drove. I would tell them all the time, "I will know before, during, or right after whatever you do." I believe it made them think twice, most of the time.

I know my trust issues must have made my daughter crazy. As an over-protective mother bear, I didn't trust anyone she wanted to spend time with. I use to tell her the red flags were flying, which meant something was off. I could not always pinpoint it, but I knew as soon as I met a person if a red flag went up or not. Most of the time, I was right and she would come to me later and say so. Then, she learned to just start asking me, "Any red flags?" Now it is Luke's turn to experience the crazy over-protective mother bear.

I liked Julie's husband when we first met him. Of course, that was because their relationship began as just friends. However, when they started dating, I wasn't so sure. Parents are never sure about the people that are dating their children. No one is ever good enough. Buddy and I began praying that God would change Julie's heart or ours. Well, He definitely changed ours. I tell everyone I didn't lose a daughter when they got married, I gained a son. I am so proud of both of them and know they are going to have a strong, happy marriage. I'm thankful she has found a man who loves and respects her. It is exciting to find that one person who knows all your flaws, mistakes, and weaknesses and still thinks you are completely amazing. God knows that about us and thinks we are amazing. The person you marry should know it, as well.

She was an absolutely beautiful bride on her wedding day. It happened too quickly for me, but I am so proud of her today. She has turned into a strong, brave, smart woman. Of course, I wish they were closer to home. She has experienced some big adjustments with leaving home and moving across the country. When she starts feeling down, I always remind her of the Winnie the Pooh quote she loved growing up, "Promise me you'll always remember: you're braver than you believe, and stronger than you seem, and smarter than you think" (A. A. Milne).

Our son, Luke, has such a kind heart. He is always worried about others. He is also our source of humor. We can always count on him to make us laugh, either on purpose or not. It definitely would be boring around here without him. I am proud of the young godly young man he has become. It's exciting to watch him become interested in the business. I know that God has great plans for him and he will do great things in his life.

Julie has always been Luke's protector from the day he was born and she held out her arms and said, "My baby." They didn't always get along, but, I am thankful they have always loved each other and wanted to protect each other. Of course, Julie tried to protect him too much at times.

One day, Julie thought she was protecting Luke and actually locked him in the car, with the keys inside, in the middle of nowhere. We tried everything to get into the car. We went to a nearby laundromat to get a wire coat hanger. Believe it or not, they didn't have any. I was starting to panic, so we called the fire department. A single fire truck showed up, but when two elderly gentlemen emerged, and could barely walk themselves, all I could think was, "Boy, we are in trouble now."

I became frantic and was searching for something to break the window, when out of nowhere two other men appeared with a wire coat hanger. Within minutes, they had the car door open. I was so relieved when I was able to get my hands on Luke; all I could do was hold him tight.

By the time I turned around to thank our rescuers, they were gone. I truly believe they were angels, as described in Hebrews 13:2: "Be not forgetful to entertain strangers: for thereby some have entertained angels unawares."

We have always strived to make memories with our kids by planning at least one big family trip every year, usually during the Christmas break. Most of the time, we went on a big hunt somewhere. I have plenty of animal-related mementos around my home to remind us of those great trips. We also have the humor from all those trips that make us laugh until we are crying every time we think about them. We have experienced everything from rest stop humor to cabin fever. Boy, the things you can see at rest stops. One time, we saw a little old lady emerging from a bathroom with a long string of toilet paper trailing behind her, and every time her poor husband tried to help her, she kept swatting him away. He finally threw his hands up.

We laugh today about our Mario Brothers wars. We played Mario on the Gameboys against each other; good-naturedly declaring that whoever was winning obviously must have been cheating. It usually ended with someone upset or crying, and Buddy threatening to throw them out the window. It was always a good time.

During our first deer photo session—yes, they have photo sessions with the deer. We always hunted with an outfitter, and they wanted pictures for advertising. Julie and I were laughing so hard during our first experience that we had to walk away. Here were these grown men setting the deer up in position using rocks and sticks, whatever they could find. They walked back to the truck and got a large box of baby wipes to clean the deer up. Then they pull out combs to brush them down. Oh, and we cannot forget the glass eyes. It was quite humorous to watch them, but the pictures turned out well.

To give you an example of Luke's humor, he always had an interesting way of pronouncing different words. Lafayette was "laugh Eddie" and Haagen-Dazs ice cream was "hanging days." The best "Luke story" of all has to be the time we were on a long hunting trip with lots of driving and early mornings. One evening, while we were getting settled in for the night, Luke asked me, "What are the symptoms of cabin fever?"

It took everything I had to not start laughing because to him the question was a serious one.

I said, "Son, why do you ask?"

He replied, "Well I'm not feeling too well, and I think I might be catching it." He was so serious we couldn't laugh at him.

We talk about the different hunts all the time and will always cherish those memories. I know Julie will never forget the year that she and Buddy went on a two-week turkey hunt all by themselves. They drove from Florida to South Dakota, making stops on the way back home. I am thankful that we were able to spend that time with our kids.

"Everyday of our lives we make deposits in the memory banks of our children." –Chuck Swindoll

Through times of both hardship and success, we have tried to remain humble. We wanted to raise our kids to respect others and never think they were better than anyone else. They learned to work for the things they wanted, which helped them to be more appreciative, and feel a sense of accomplishment through the fruits of their labors. They raised steers, which they showed and sold each year at the county fair. They were always so excited when their checks came in the mail. We would sit down and figure out their tithe for the church. They always wanted to pick a special missionary project to send money to in addition to their tithes. Usually, they came up with something they wanted to buy and would share in the expense, and then the rest would go into their savings. By the time they were both sixteen, they bought their own vehicle. We have really tried to teach them to work for everything they get. It makes me proud that they always had the desire to help with a missionary project every year. God blesses us so that we can bless others. This truth can be summed up in the following quote by Chuck Swindoll, which aired on his radio program, "Insight for Living":

God has assigned all Christians various responsibilities that correspond to the talents He has given us. Some of us are two-talent people, some are four-talent people, and most of us are one-talent servants. God always gives us exactly what we can handle and enough to fulfill the role He wants us to fill. But it's our choice whether we share His blessings and talents with others or hoard them for ourselves.

We all want to be able to leave something to our kids. A lot of people focus on making more money and acquiring more things to leave an inheritance to their children. Our real legacy should go way beyond the material things we leave behind. Our legacy should have a powerful influence on the lives of those around us. The most important legacies are the emotional, spiritual and moral impacts we leave with others as we encounter them on our life's journey. The ultimate blessing we can give our children is teaching them to love the Lord and serve Him.

> For he established a testimony in Jacob, and appointed a law in Israel, which he commanded our fathers, that they should make them known to their children: That the generation to come might know them, even the children which should be born; who should arise and declare them to their children. -Psalm 78:5-6

I recently heard a lady say, "You are not 'just' anything. Whatever you are doing is important to someone, even if you feel like it is small or unimportant." You are not "just" a mom, wife, or whatever. You are important. What you do is important to you and those who share your life with you. Those words struck a chord within me because I catch myself saying those words all the time:

- "I am 'just' Buddy's wife."
- "I am 'just' Julie and Luke's mom."

No, I am honored to be Buddy's wife and I am honored to be Julie and Luke's mom. God gave each of them to me, and I should treat it as the highest honor to be able to serve and love my husband and children. I didn't come to this realization overnight, but it was revealed to me as I studied what the Word of God has to say about taking spiritual pride in serving our family, friends, and community – there is nothing lowly about serving in the name of Christ. The seemingly small things we do for others often mean the most to them, and we should not take it lightly, for in doing for others we are serving the Lord.

The examples of a servant's heart are found in many Biblical passages, but the greatest example was Jesus, the King of Heaven, who came to earth and washed the feet of His disciples, illustrating to them and us the importance of true service in the name of God. The Biblical examples are endless: the story of Martha and Mary, the woman who washed the feet of Jesus and dried them with her hair, the disciples who left everything to follow Jesus, and so on. These provided me with insight, and also taught me to seek answers from scripture, for when we truly seek truth, God will lead us to it. Even on those days when others may not appreciate our efforts, the knowledge that we are working for Christ allows us to serve wholeheartedly and let Him do the work in the hearts of others.

"And whatsoever ye do, do it heartily, as to the Lord, and not unto men; knowing that of the Lord ye shall receive the reward of the inheritance: for ye serve the Lord Christ." – Colossians 2:23 – 24

Chapter 6

UNWAVERING

I'm thankful to God for my salvation and for directing my path daily. I'm thankful for His unwavering love for me. I'm blessed by some amazing people He has placed in my life. It seems like the right person always showed up at the right time in my life. I continue to learn from their struggles and diligent efforts to triumph over seemingly insurmountable challenges. They help me to strive everyday to be a better person.

***

First, there is my "Superman," as I call him -- my loving, supportive husband. We have definitely had our ups and downs through the years. We had a rough start, but since the day we married he has always stood by my side. He is a dedicated father to our two kids and loves unconditionally. I watch him fight every day for our family and the many families that depend upon him. Does he get frustrated? Absolutely. There are many days when he wants to quit, but he always finds that mustard seed of faith to keep going, because he knows that he is ultimately working for the Lord. Buddy doesn't like the word, "can't". I hear him say to our kids and employees, "Can't never could and won't never will." Of course, our kids now finish the quote before he does! Another of his famous quotes is, "Quitters never win and winners never quit." He definitely lives both of these truths and inspires others with his testimony of faith and reliance upon God. Although he has had all the "nay-sayers" throughout his life trying to knock him down, he always finds the strength to continue on. I know it is his deep faith in God that gets him through, but it is still hard for me to watch him struggle at times. He is always available to encourage someone else and put others first. Even when he is at his lowest point, he walks around with the weight of the world on his shoulders with a smile. I look at all he does for our family and everyone else and it amazes me. I believe God has blessed him and our family above and beyond our imagination because of his faithfulness. I never pictured my life as it is now. Is he perfect? No, but he is perfect for our family and me. He is our "Superman."

***

My children are such a blessing to me. I'm thankful that God allowed me the opportunity to be their mom. It has been one of my greatest joys. I'm a better person because of them. It thrills my heart to see them both active in church and loving the Lord.

***

I am thankful for my family. My mom taught me how to work hard and always keep going. She always worked hard to take care of us kids. She didn't accept any government help, and I don't remember her ever complaining. I know she had a lot to deal with emotionally; who wouldn't feel overwhelmed when a husband of seventeen years walks out and leaves you to care for four kids by yourself?

While I was growing up, I never recall her speaking badly about my father to us. As a matter of fact, I remember her making excuses for him. I know this must have required a great deal of courage and fortitude on her part, and I admire her for it. As I got older, I felt like a burden to her. She didn't make me feel that way; I just saw how hard she worked and felt bad that I couldn't do more to help. It goes back to those "everything is my fault" feelings I believed about myself until God taught me about forgiving myself, as well as others.

Looking back, I realize that my mom did all she could, and then some, for her kids, which gives me the drive to do my best for my own children. My siblings and I are all adults now and have managed to put our own mirrors back together.

We all have busy lives and don't get to see each other often, but I hope they all know how much I love them. None of us are perfect and we may let each other down at times, but I try to remember that everyone is looking through their mirror and may not see the same images as I, so we have to forgive, move forward, and try to do better. They all have their own stories to tell as they gaze into their individual mirrors. I can't tell you their perspective, but I have learned from each of them and their lives.

***

My best friend is one of the most passionate and dedicated women I know. I have watched her for the past several years, raising and caring for a special needs child with unwavering love and devotion. Her drive and determination to improve her son's life inspires everyone who knows her. I don't know how she manages to keep everything going—balancing the needs of her exceptional teenager along with a younger son, graduating from nursing school, and helping her husband with his business. How she does it, I don't know. Her example has made me a more thoughtful person because of having a remarkable individual, like her, in my life. Her precious little boy has also inspired my daughter to go to college and major in Exceptional Student Education.

***

I have what I joyously refer to as "my adopted dad." We have no official papers, but this man has truly showed me a father's love. One day at church, I was having a difficult time. I believe it was around Father's Day. I made a comment to him that sometimes it would just be nice to have a father to seek advice since my real father was no longer in the picture. He replied to me that I could come to him whenever I needed. He may regret that offer some days, because I have definitely called on him many times. He has always tried to help.

I was not only blessed with a "dad" but also another "mom" and another older sister to look up to. They have been a great encouragement to my kids and me. My adopted sister has been one of my biggest cheerleaders in writing this book by helping me put all my random thoughts in some order so that it could be read. This wonderful family I've been adopted into has taught me about unconditional love because they accept me even though I am not a blood relative. I can say that I have felt a father's love again and a void has been filled. It was a proud moment to see him and his lovely wife on the front row watching my daughter -- their granddaughter -- get married. No, they are not perfect either. They do display a great example of what a loving Christian marriage ought to be.

***

My church family, as well as the pastor and his family, have helped me to see that God's people can show God's love. There are so many people in the church that have encouraged us and just shown us their love. The pastor and his wife are close to our hearts. Their kids were a little older than ours, so my kids looked up to them and spent time with them. They were close. Our pastor's wife is also one of my best friends. She is always there for me and I try to always be there for her. She never judges me, but is also quick to lovingly tell me when she sees something wrong. We tend to get ourselves involved in many projects. In the middle of these projects, we always call ourselves crazy for starting them. "What were we thinking?" is the usual comment. Though we can always count on each other to find another crazy project to start.

***

Both sets of my grandparents have had a huge impact on my life. Before my father left, we spent many summers in the Florida Keys,with his parents. I have many great memories of my time there, even though I got seasick almost every time we went out in the boat. I believe my grandfather fed me a huge breakfast so I could chum the fish for him. The house we own now in The Keys is only a short distance from where they lived. It has been neat to revisit the area and remember old times.

I remember spending many summers and vacations with my mom's parents. My grandfather had a tough and gruff appearance, but he showed his love to us. My grandfather, Col. Marcell ("Marc") Emery Fountain, US Air Force, was the pilot aboard a B-25 Bomber, nicknamed the "Royal Flush". They were shot down on one of their missions. He was sent to a German concentration camp in Stalag Luft III from June 22, 1943 until forced to march to Moosburg, Germany on January 27, 1945. He remained at Stalag 7A, in Moosburg, until freed by the Americans on April 29, 1945.

He came home from Germany and still continued to serve his country. He saw his share of many wars and conflicts. I remember him helping me with a school project about WWII. How painful it must have been for him to recount those experiences, but he actually sat down with me and helped me draw maps of the Death March. He is the definition of a true hero.

***

I have recently read a book titled, Fearless: The Undaunted Courage and Ultimate Sacrifice of Navy SEAL Team Six Operator Adam Brown by Eric Blehm. It is an amazing testimony of family and a true American hero.

I just cannot stop talking about the impact it has had on me. I have always had great respect for the military, because I have family that served and some are still serving. After reading this book, I have a whole new respect for them now, especially for the Navy SEALs and their families. They might sacrifice their life in death, but their family undergoes serious sacrifices during the entire period of service. They say goodbye many times not knowing if it will be their last goodbye. Every time families go to the gate at the airport to pick them up, they are just thankful their loved ones are alive and have returned home to them.

Not only did the military side of the book grab my attention, but Eric's testimony for God is amazing. His strength, courage, and perseverance originate from his faith in the Lord. He was not shy about sharing his faith with others - he wanted them to know the good, bad and the ugly aspects about his life. Eric's life illustrates that we should not be afraid to share our lives with others.

Reading this book has given me the encouragement to share my story. Even while writing, I was hesitant on how much to share. What would people think of me? After reading Adam's story and praying long and hard, I know God wants me to share my testimony. He wants me out of my comfort zone so I can grow. My desire for this book is that it will point straight back to Jesus and what He can do in the lives of those that submit to His will.

"But sanctify the Lord God in your hearts: and be ready always to give an answer to every man that asketh you a reason of the hope that is in you with meekness and fear." – 1 Peter 3:15

Chapter 7

MY MIRROR TODAY

When our inner mirror is whole and unbroken, it is similar to water on a lake. We can look into each of these and see a clear reflection looking back at us. When our mirror breaks or a rock gets thrown into the lake, stirring the water, the image we see becomes blurry. That is when the fairytale world we like to create falls apart and we start to see all the negative things around us. We tend to focus on the physical more than the spiritual. It is easier to pick apart the physical, seeing ourselves as not pretty or skinny enough, or give into the temptation of attacking someone else, blaming them for all our problems. If we focus on the spiritual, then we have to align ourselves up to God. This requires us to make changes in our life and sometimes those changes can be hard and uncomfortable.

Prior to my salvation and before I learned to rely on God's promises, the only reflection I saw was an angry person. I was mad at everyone in my life that had left or hurt me. I had no desire for forgiveness or reconciliation. I was a bitter and sad person. I didn't feel as though I could do anything right, or that I was good enough for anyone to love. I didn't trust anyone. How could anyone love me when I didn't even like myself?

Even after salvation, it has been a constant battle to rid myself of all the ugly thought patterns. God forgives us, but we have to be willing to let go and not let it drag us back down into the pit, where the devil tries to lure us. We have to learn to claim the strength in the scriptures. In Isaiah 43:1-3, it tells us that God knows us by name and promises to walk with us. He does not promise it will be easy or painless. We just have to be willing to lean on His words for comfort and strength to endure.

But now thus saith the Lord that created thee, "O Jacob, and he that formed thee, O Israel, Fear not: for I have redeemed thee, I have called thee by thy name; thou art mine. When thou passest through the waters, I will be with thee; and through the rivers, they shall not overflow thee: when thou walkest through the fire, thou shalt not be burned; neither shall the flame kindle upon thee. For I am the Lord thy God, the Holy One of Israel, thy Saviour: I gave Egypt for thy ransom, Ethiopia and Seba for thee." – Isaiah 43:1-3

The reflection I see today is not as blurry—but it's not always clear. It is definitely a work in progress. I have been a huge project for God. I tried to interfere with His plans for my life for a long time. I definitely experience more peace when I allow God to work though.

I know that I am loved -- first by God, and then by my family. I have learned the true meaning of love. I've also learned how to forgive. It's not always easy, but forgiveness is essential. I no longer see myself as completely broken - just not completely mended yet. I have to continue working and striving to be what God wants. I know I will mess up. We all mess up our lives when we decide to do our own thing and not wait on the Lord. Then, we think we can hide it from Him, when all we have to do is go to God and ask for His forgiveness. He will take us and remold us so that we can start living for Him again. That is His wonderful promise to us.

"But now, O Lord, thou art our father; we are the clay, and thou our potter; and we all are the work of thy hand."–Isaiah 64:8

I am so thankful that God continues to pick me up and dust me off. There are a lot of times that I have let people down and hurt them. I am forever grateful to those who forgave me and allowed me to move forward. They will never know how much it meant to me. The feeling of being forgiven by someone you have wronged is a close second to Jesus's forgiveness.

> "Forbearing one another, and forgiving one another, if any man have a quarrel against any: even as Christ forgave you, so also do ye" – (Colossians 3:13).

Our deepest emotional need is to feel loved. Sometimes we want the other person to do something first to earn our love. We have to remember that God put the desire to love first within us. He is our example. God loved us when we were sinful, unresponsive, and had done nothing to earn His love. That is the ultimate example of love. This is the kind of love we should strive for in our marriage and all other relationships in our lives. We have to learn to seek spiritual fulfillment instead of relying on someone or something to fulfill us.

> "In this was manifested the love of God toward us, because that God sent his only begotten Son into the world, that we might live through him. Herein is love, not that we loved God, but that he loved us, and sent his Son to be the Propitiation for our sins. Beloved, if God so loved us, we ought also love one another." – 1 John 4:9-11

When we feel overwhelmed with everything thrown at us, we must remember we are just managing blessings.

We have to find the good in everything. Even when things look bad, God has a blessing in it for us. God does not always change the circumstances -- sometimes He just wants to change us.

During various times of problems and inconveniences, I have learned to lean on God; He is the only one who satisfies completely. People will let us down, but He never will. He allows situations and circumstances to occur in our lives in order to bring us closer to Him.

We have to remember there is a difference between problems and inconveniences. A major life threatening illness is a problem. Losing our car keys is an inconvenience. Sometimes those minor inconveniences have prevented a major problem. How many times have you been delayed and it prevented you from being involved in an accident or something potentially catastrophic?

God is always watching us and protecting us. We just have to learn to be sensitive to His will. I have learned that God will never leave His children, even when we turn our backs on Him. When things feel out of control, don't worry. God has your back. Just remember the words in Psalm 120:1. He is always listening.

"In my distress I cried unto the Lord, and he heard me." –Psalm 120:1

During one of my journaling classes, there was a part where we picked three key words that we desired. Joy, love, and safety were mine. I believe God has blessed me with all of those today. He has given me the desires of my heart.

Joy – I have joy in my life because of Jesus. I may not always be happy, but I can lean on Jesus and find joy. Trying to learn to be joyful no matter what is going on is a work in progress.

Love – I didn't know the true meaning of love until I accepted Jesus into my life. He is our greatest example. I also have the love of my friends and family and I have truly experienced unconditional love with Buddy.

Safety – The biggest part of the feeling of safety was letting go of fear. Fear will paralyze you. I have learned to trust God and Buddy completely. I know God will never leave me nor forsake me and Buddy has shown me over and over again he is committed to our marriage.

"Delight thyself also in the Lord: and he shall give thee the desires of thine heart" – (Psalm 37:4).

Laughter is a necessity in our lives and our marriages. I have always been one who laughed at awkward times. Times when I probably should have been crying. I know my kids remember me saying, "We have to laugh so we won't cry." I guess it is a defense mechanism. One example was when I was seven months pregnant with Julie, I was involved in an accident. I was really scared and wanted to cry, but as soon as I got on the phone with Buddy, all I could do was laugh. He knew he'd better hurry.

Laughter is also just good for the soul. It makes for a fun, happy marriage when you can laugh together. There are many studies about how laughter is good for your health. Long before these studies, we had scripture to tell us the same thing. God is pretty awesome.

"A merry heart doeth good like a medicine: but a broken spirit drieth the bones."–Proverbs 17:22

Sometimes life is tough and we want to give up, but we have to stay focused on what we are living for. We must remember to strive after Godly prosperity not material prosperity. As long as we continue to do for the Lord, and not ourselves, we should never stop growing in our Christian walk. Problems come into play when desires turn from godly desires into selfish ones. It is the desire of my and Buddy's heart to be able to say, "I have fought a good fight, I have finished my course, I have kept the faith" (2 Timothy 4:7).

In the drawing together of our lives and how we serve God with fellow believers, Buddy and I are encouraged by Romans 15:5-6, where Paul tells us, "Now the God of patience and consolation grant you to be likeminded one toward another according to Christ Jesus: that ye may with one mind and one mouth glorify God, even the Father of our Lord Jesus Christ."

God has also revealed to me that growth comes by wisdom. We must humbly ask for wisdom when seeking His will for our lives. God will provide a light for our journey. He will turn us from our selfishness of gazing into the mirrors of ourselves, and point us instead to the mirrors found within the Bible, which reflect how to lead a Christian life. Neither Buddy nor I knew about these things until God intervened in our lives and revealed them to us.

"My brethren, count it all joy when ye fall into divers temptations; knowing this, that the trying of your faith worketh patience. But let patience have her perfect work, that ye may be perfect and entire, wanting nothing. If any of you lack wisdom, let him ask of God, that giveth to all men liberally, and upbraideth not; and it shall be given him. But let him ask in faith, nothing wavering. For he that wavereth is like a wave of the sea driven with the wind and tossed. For let not that man think that he shall receive any thing of the Lord. A double-minded man is unstable in all his ways." – James 1:2-8

Growing, learning, and seeking wisdom on a daily basis is difficult. We are faced with the challenges of everyday living, and combating selfish desires daily. It is only through God's unfailing power that we find victory. These revelations have come to us the hard way. Whenever we tried to do anything under our own power and our own abilities, God reminded us that He is ultimately in control. Growing up amid turmoil in our childhoods, we had difficulty trusting our lives to an unseen God. As you have read through the story of our journey, you have seen how He patiently guided us, often without us even knowing it. I pray that you will let God guide you so you can see amazing things happen in your life also.

We are still on this crazy ride and things change all the time. We are now starting to reorganize our lives and downsize. Our new motto is, "less is more." With Julie married and on her own and Luke almost at that age, we felt it was time. We have sold the ranch and will be moving into a smaller home we have built on a lake. We are excited about what God has in store for us as we continue to serve Him.

"Whereunto I also labour, striving according to his working, which worketh in me mightily."
–Colossians 1:29

As far as my mirror today? Well, like I said earlier, some days it is clearer than others. I have to strive everyday to follow God and allow Him to work in my life. Every new day is a day to find an opportunity to serve Him and show His love to others. I am looking forward to the day when my mirror will be completely whole again -- the day Jesus comes back.

"For our conversation is in heaven; from whence also we look for the Saviour, the Lord Jesus Christ: Who shall change our vile body, that it may be fashioned like unto his glorious body, according to the working whereby he is able even to subdue all things unto himself." – Philippians 3:20-21

CPSIA information can be obtained at www.ICGtesting.com
Printed in the USA
LVOW04s0607150115

422830LV00003B/5/P